Café Crazy

Café Crazy

Poems by

Francine Witte

Kelsay Books

© 2018 Francine Witte. All rights reserved. This material may not be reproduced in any form, published, reprinted, recorded, performed, broadcast, rewritten or redistributed without the explicit permission of Francine Witte. All such actions are strictly prohibited by law.

Cover: Patrick McConahay

ISBN: 13: 978-1-947465-32-9

Kelsay Books
Aldrich Press
www.kelsaybooks.com

Acknowledgments

Grateful acknowledgement is made to the editors of the following journals, in which some of these poems were first published:

Barbaric Yawp, Black Fox Literary Review, Bryant Literary Review, Calliope, Careless Embrace of the Boneshaker, Cloudbank, Crab Creek Review, Evening Street Review, Front Range Review, Harpur's Palate, Hawaii Pacific Review, Home Planet News, Kentucky Review, LIPS, *MacGuffin, Moon City Review, Nimrod, Not All Fires Burn the Same* Chapbook, NYSAI, *Paterson Literary Review, Pinyon, Poet's Billow, Saranac Review, Skidrow Penthouse, Slant, Slippery Elm, Southeast Review, Two Bridges Review, Willow Review, Wisconsin Review,*

A loving thank you to my husband, Mark, for his unwavering support of my writing.

A special thanks to George Wallace for his sharp editorial help on this manuscript.

And eternal thanks to Lori Schimmel Drucker, my sweet and darling sister, who passed away this summer. I miss you every day.

Contents

Not All Fires Burn the Same	11
Earth Before Us	12
Overall Light	13
Charley Says Give Me Your Heart	14
Story of My Life	16
Tomato Scream	18
By the Time I'm Born	19
Atlantic City Boardwalk, 1949	20
Convenience	22
Learning to Trust Your Gut	24
All the Babies	25
One Night, Charley	26
Turning	27
There was a Time	28
Nights Like That	29
Charley Explains Baseball to Me	30
Whoosh	31
Not Only	32
Breaking Sky	33
Stormbrew	35
Divorce on Mars	36
Wednesday	37
Selfie at the End of the World	39
December was a Bad Idea	40
What Started as Fun	41
Bleed	42
When Charley Goes James Dean on Me	43
Wife	44
That was the Summer	45
Give Me Back	46
Other Charlies	47
Then	48

Mother-in-Law	49
Flight	50
Pumpkin School	51
Probably	52
Dusk	53
Charley Gives Me an Either/Or	54
When We Meet Up at the Parker Avenue Grill	55
I Think of My Mother	56
Daughter in the Kitchen	58
Roses	59
In My Poems, Sometimes I Have Children	60
My Sister Is Dying	61
Love was Okay	62
Fish Story	63
Even in the Shark World	64
Shark Week!	65
When Charley Starts to Look Like the Weather	67
Years Later	68
Question for Jessica	69
Poem Where Charley Gets It in the Gut	71
For Barbara	72
Status	73
On My Way Away	74
Charley Leaves Me in a Swamp	75
Café Crazy	76

About the Author

Not All Fires Burn the Same

Take the ones on the evening news,
forest scorch, flames like wolf tongues.
You are watching, safe behind your TV tray,
feeling smug and oh so cool. Not at all
like those fires you started as a kid, stolen
matches, newspaper in the sink. Sparks
flying under the cabinets, and you could have
burned the kitchen down. But that
was nothing like the fire of your husband
and his other woman, how you thought
he should be strong enough to reason
her away. You didn't see his fingers
and how burnt they already were. Dark
and scarred as that TV forest you thought
was so far off, where the fire had to eat
its fill before it could go home. And when
your husband finally limped back to you,
hands full of dead smoke and regret,
you let him into your lukewarm
bed. And when he kissed you, you
could taste the ashes still in his mouth.

Earth Before Us

with its unwalked paths,
its undug soil, and all that
unbreathed air. There were
holes that man would later
fill. Spaces trying to close,

but couldn't. The animals
knew it. Could smell the futuresmoke
of burnt forests. Fish, too, could feel
the weight of the ocean, still heavy
on their backs, before

the steel hooks pierced
their flappy flesh. Back then,
the whole world was like a strong
hand holding it all in place, a tightened
grasp that would be pried apart the minute
the first human eye popped open.

Overall Light

Above all this, above the flat roads
hooded by willows, above the souped-up
shadows that buildings cast, above
all this there is light, the first command
that God gave—light,
switched on, flooding
the universe, that debut
of stars so that eons later,
astronauts walking in space,
stabbing small cuts
in the darkness, would know
which way to aim. Light.
Your eyes when somebody
tells you they love you. Light.
What you turn from ending the day.

Listen, historians know nothing
but this: the past
is a scatter behind us.
History is just what got lit.

Charley Says Give Me Your Heart

It is gentle,
and I want to know it.

First thought is run,
but I've been alone

so many months.
I stretch

my arms to see
if they still reach

another human being.
And they do.

Charley says
put out the light,

and he swoops down
with a force

even time
doesn't have.

I'm a young girl
compared to the Earth,

and I've see animals
shred each other's skin

in the name of hunger,
the crime everyone forgives.

Next morning, light
tears me up like a canine tooth.

I am alone,
although Charley is here.

He turns to me
and simply says, give me your heart.

It is mine now,
and later,

I might
want it.

Story of My Life

Born. Maybe wanted. Maybe
not. Later, I learn how I started,
a lick of perfume
on my mother's virgin throat.

Soon, I'm too big to carry,
so my mother sets me down.
I walk and walk,
end up 25 years from home,

taking the slow steps of a blind man,
no cane. "Who are you?"
I ask, "friend?" No
answer. I say

"please take me home," and
a voice says "where's home?"
Here, I stop cold
as the afternoon sun
sinks down its jaw.

"Home is the direction
I'm going," I say
all bravado, no shame.
Meanwhile, dark keeps coming on
like a bully's fist,
backs me up

against the wall.
Times like this,
I'll promise anything, mean
it, too. This will be a good year,

I say. The one I've been wishing
towards all of my life. But first
things first. Let's go back,
write things down this time,
so everyone knows I've got it

right. Now, see that woman
pushing pebbles back
into the pavement with every
step, face brazen
into the sun? She's who I'm gonna be
ten years ago.

Tomato Scream

I'm eating my salad when Charley says—
how do you know tomatoes
can't feel? How do you really
know anything? I know *this:*

when Charley gets metaphorical,
it's time to hide the wine.
Yesterday, it was roof sag
and how do you expect a bunch

of shingles to hold up
all that snow? What he meant
was—how can I ever match

your expectations? Funny. I thought
I told him long ago that I'd be happy
with one quiet night after another.
Quit the booze, and everything

falls into place. So simple.
Like algebra, unless you were sleeping
in class that day. Me?

I'm more of a simile girl.
Charley watches me eat my salad.
His eyes go cloudy as a Bloody Mary.
I stab the tomato. It oozes like a wound.

By the Time I'm Born

all kinds of history has happened.
Wars and extinctions and
continental drift. What is
it anyone thinks that I have
to add? Sure, if I were a
dinosaur, say, or a woolly
mammoth, I could be
happy for my brief stay
on Earth, a tick on this
mossy garden oozing
with steamy amoeba soup
and a meteor headed my way.

But the fact is, we don't
know what's out there, and so we go
along futurestupid. We worry about
the little things, which countries
are glaring at each other, and what
are the chances of a nuclear slip?
Focus further, let's really microscope
this thing, and it's crazy what we have
time for. Fashion and baseball and God
knows what. So really adorable to think
that we have some hidden secret the
dinosaurs missed, and that everything
we touch or want, even the greatest loves
of our lives will just go on forever, without
us even thinking to check our watch.

Atlantic City Boardwalk, 1949

This photograph wants to be still,
but instead, it keeps turning into

an almost-live tableau. Take my mother,
for example. Newlywed young, she is waving

at the camera in what could be hello
or goodbye. I would love to ask her,

that's how real she seems. I feel like
I might have known her, but, of course,

I never did. Never knew this happy girl
or the sad, wordless woman she would end

up to be, when I saw her at the nursing home
and had to keep telling her my name, the name

she once told me she chose because it reminded
her of France. Beside her is my father, fedora-handsome,

his arm protective around her, as if shielding her from
the ocean spray and the man he would one day

become. Standing around them, my four grandparents,
all of them younger than I am now. Overcoats

and permanents, they huddle close against the autumn
chill. The ocean, a backdrop behind them,

open and possible. They are smiling, maybe the taste

of salt-spray in their mouths. I wait for them to somehow break out
of their frame and come towards me, but instead

they just stand there, almost as if they are watching
me back, as if waiting to see if I will break

out of the pose I am standing in now.

Convenience

Suppose it's Thursday, and you're driving home
from picking up your husband, who decided
he didn't feel like bowling after all, like he usually
does. *No reason*, he says, and you know better

than to ask. You pull into the parking lot.
Milk for tomorrow's breakfast. Morning will
smack the sun back in the sky, and your husband
will be yours again for a while. By the time
you're in the dairy aisle, you're certain he's texting

his girlfriend. Phase-out stage, and you know this
by the way he's been nuzzling you in the middle
of the night. Just like the last time. And the time
before that. And as soon as you dropped
your guard, he was done with you

again. Now, you pick up a carton of milk,
check the expiration. Good for another day.
Outside, the girl is probably texting back
What's wrong, or *what did I do?* He will
tell her *nothing*, the way he'll be
telling you a month from now.

You want to hate this girl, find her name
in his unguarded cell and track her like a dog.
But the truth is, you're as bad as she is,
loving a no-good man, unable to walk away.
You feel more like a painsister
than a wounded wife, and when

you step back into the parking lot, see him
stashing his phone in his pocket, sliding
into the driver's seat, you know again
that a carton of milk is all
you can admit to needing.

Learning to Trust Your Gut

Remember that first you are
an animal, reacting in animal
ways. Your nostrils flare at predators.
Your eyes squint you out of the sun.
Your body tells you everything. You know
all this. You've always known. But still,
you have doubts. You button a blouse
over a twinge in your belly, smooth lipstick
over a quivering lip. You teach yourself
to adjust. And when alarms go off,
blaring you out of a burning building,
you learn to breathe shallow, or step
around the flames. You know a lie
in a whisper, or taste goodbye
in a kiss. But you have magazines stacked
to the ceiling telling you to ignore
the flutter inside your bones. Listen,
your heart's in a cage for a reason. It's
a prisoner banging up against the walls,
scraping a cup along the bars,
just waiting for someone to hear.

All the Babies

I could have been. Take, for example,
my mother's first boyfriend. Sweaty,
geometry hands. *Well, someone had
to date him*, she would later say. I
liked her for that, but I was happy
he wasn't my father. Or the next one,
Hank, a nice boy, but sick. Epilepsy,
my mother would whisper. Anyway,
he died six months later. Suicide,
though she couldn't say the word.
But, then, there was my father, handsome
stranger. *Roseland* on a restless August night.
They went out once, and he didn't call
back. She told me she was ready
to let it go. But maybe I was
in the air around her head. Wordless
spirit hovering as she sat there, ignored.
Nudging her against her better judgement,
pushing her invisibly to pick up that phone.

One Night, Charley

goes moonstupid and pops out
a ring. *I'm trying something,* he says

like it's a suit or a new car. Me,
I've been picturing this moment,

but it wasn't like this. No tablecloths
or candles. No roaming violins. And, frankly,

after all this time, Charley down on one knee
looks like he's tying his shoe. *Get up,*

I tell him. And then I tell him I'm happy
like we are. No pressure, no having

to be anyone's forever. The way we are
is one step after another. *Bites of an elephant,*

I say. But he's already gone. Face in the fuck-
you position. Scrunched up mouth and eyes

that won't meet mine. Charley snaps the ring
back in its box. Angry clamshell. *I thought*

you'd be happy, he finally says. I think of trying
to make him understand, but really it's

like what comedians says about a joke,
if you have to explain it, it wasn't funny.

Turning

The angels are flying south
for the winter, my father said,
pointing to the fast-moving clouds.

Just yesterday, they were the cotton,
leftover from when God made bunnies.
I wanted to tell him it's the birds

that fly south and that angels don't feel
winter, and that bunnies are made of flesh
and fur, and there's nothing about them

that they don't need. But that was
the moment my father became a person
to me, separate and on his way to dying,

already sinking into his own skin.
And me, seeing the last sands
of my childhood, not ready

to let go, just looked up at the sky,
told him the angels are beautiful,
as beautiful as the people they

once used to be.

There was a Time

when the earth was flat,
ironed out to the edges, and

if you traveled far enough,
you'd simply fall off, get

swallowed up in some open
spacejaw. This was how

it was, until one day, the scientists
said no, and even worse, proved it

with measured shadows and inconsistent stars.
Soon, there were divisions, camps

of believers and non. Possible brothers
who had suckled at the same breast,

now shunning one another. Maybe lovers
arguing, the air hissing out of their balloon-y

relationships. Love itself going flat.
And yes, it's easy for us now,

to laugh at their tiny mindsets,
and give ourselves a collective nod

as we sip on our café lattes
some dressed with foam, some not.

Nights Like That

there were secrets, whispers.
Your parents next door
in the living room,
grownup mumbles. We
were ten then, and you
told me what boys like
to do. *It's like baseball*,

you said, *but it's not
baseball*. We were best
friends, and no one knew
how young you would die.

We could hear your parents
through the thin walls.
Your father whooshing open
a beer. Your mother saying "don't."
That's when you told
me that first base

was a kiss and that Susie Wallace
from the sixth grade, let a boy
get to second. I must have
cried out, disbelief,

because that's when your mother
swooshed in, tried to shush
us down. Too late, genie unbottled,
I would never be the same.

And you? Your eyes were flinching
from the sudden light let in
from the living room, the shadow
behind you on the wall, winding
up its arm to pitch.

Charley Explains Baseball to Me

and how it's about history,
game six and Gehrig and so many

stats. I tell Charley that history
hasn't been kind to him and me,

and I remind him about the night
he hooked up with the ice cream girl,

and how I forgave him because booze
was already the other woman. Of course,

I say this only in my head. Charley stopped
listening long ago. And I think about leaving again,

and again, I think how easy life could be, clean,
as the smack of a bat or a baseball birding

through the sky. And that's when Charley
tells me how he could've gone pro. Star catcher

in the pee-wee league, and later scouted
in high school, but the damn drink hooked him

early. Easy fish. He takes a deep breath
and says he'll tell me more later.

I settle back in for the evening, looking
at the boy that lives in Charley's face.

Whoosh

Sometimes, the river clenches and boats rise
and rocks lower into the waterskin and trees
bow and shimmy in the wind, and the wind is weak
compared to the brush of your coat as you leave
the party early, and the host smiles at you like a player
piano rolling out the tune of let's have lunch
and safe trip home, and he doesn't know how
you just saw goodbye looming in your lover's
eyes, a casual glance as he handed you a gin
and tonic and looked the other way, but you
felt the water rising and the trees lowering
and all of it coming towards you like a river
all hunched up with why he could never love you,
after all, and now you are searching the parking lot
for your car and higher ground, and you know
that when you do find shelter, it will just be
for the moment, what with the future coming after
you like the host bolting out of the party, your
left-behind car keys jingling in his hand.

Not Only

was the sun a tired eye
that day, but the birds
were starting to fidget
the wind. Somewhere, a woman
was up to here with her man
and his constant disappearings.
I deserve better, she said,
as she billowed a blanket
above the bed that was only
half-slept in. Third time
this week. Love graveyard,
she thought, and that's when
she heard the birds, all of them
gone vulture now, tapping their beaks at
the window pane, hungry to gnaw
on the corpse. And rather
than hiding this one time,
she flipped out the shutters
and let in a sickness
of birds, while she,
sorry angel, stepped
out on the porch, looked up
at the bloody sun which, we can
only imagine, was trying
its hardest not to stare.

Breaking Sky

A piece of the sky breaks off
and falls into your coffee cup.

It makes you wonder how shabby
heaven might be getting, and what will

it look like when you get there, if,
in fact, you do. You spoon

the piece from your cup and hold
it between your fingers. It is perfect

and star-shaped, and you realize
that the sky was only making room,

the way your mother's belly once
made room for you. How you were

once the star she pushed out of her
body, light falling through her thighs.

And now it's your turn, time to reshape
your mouth, learn the language your

mother now speaks, where she doesn't
quite remember you and says your name

like it's a miracle or a bathroom fixture.
You know that soon the earth will have

to change, open its skin and scar itself
back around her coffin. And it's right

now that you realize that it has taken
you your entire life to learn that sometimes

you have to hold your hand across your
coffee cup to keep the sky from falling in.

Stormbrew

up above in the morning sky. Soon,
the sun will disappear like last night's
blown-out candle. Cloudbruise
and windwhisper building now,
and underneath, a wife wakes up,
alone, her heart darkened by
her husband who said he was
leaving, and don't try to change
his mind. He told her it's been coming
for a while now, and didn't she feel
the windshift in his absences and
silences, and if she had been paying attention,
surely, she would have known.
So now, she wakes in the wreckage,
disasterscape of splinters and shards
and the slowmoving smoke of

heartbreak that is curling around her neck.

Divorce on Mars

Maybe it's better there. Maybe the moon
isn't sticking its nose into every other
sentence, reminding you what's gone.
Maybe on Mars, you don't think
about the mountains ored up with memory,
bike trails tracked with first dates, grass
beds flattened from the backs of new
lovers. Divorce on Mars is a clean
thing, unpeopled as it is. No well-meaning
neighbors to tell you how much better off you are.
And best of all, divorce on Mars has
a whole, clear view of the earth, small
as a marble you could pinch in your fingers,
rather than now, spread out like it is,
in a million different directions,
all of them going nowhere.

Wednesday

Charley says Wednesday's too
schizo, and would it please make
up its mind. *Is it coming from
last week or going towards next?*

I can see the division in Charley's
eyes. Two into seven is three
and a half. *The whole damned week
is coupled off,* he says. Thursday

and Friday, gift-wrapped and tinsel,
then Saturday, Sunday, wine-soaked
and cool. Monday and Tuesday,
drudgebucket days, but at least

they have each other. Sometimes,
I feel like Wednesday. Leftover,
halved, when Charley slams out
to find the part of himself he left

in the world. Alone, I just make
dinner, mid-week mash of cornflakes
and canned soup. Even my foods
don't go. But on some of those

nights, before Charley gets home,
I prop him up, invisible. I whisper
the question, *coming or going?*
Outside the window, a goldenrod
moon is steering real-life Charley

toward whatever it is he's looking for, while back inside, here, couch cushions sink with Charley's absent weight. And me, holding my breath as I wait for his answer.

Selfie at the End of the World

Like everything else, the apocalypse
will be photographed. Duckface crumble

of skyscrapers, or the twisty scowl of the ground
giving way. Sudden, but not surprising.

You'll remember the temperature rising
and the earth pulling off its sweater

of foliage and ice. How it all seemed
so distant, but now shows up to photobomb

that last TV reporter, humanity trampling
itself in the background. No selfie stick

long enough to fit seven billion,
so instead you gather a bouquet

of faces around you, strike a pose and shoot.

December was a Bad Idea

and not because of the snow
boom muffling the house, and how
it ended our story, the story your mouth

got tired of telling, or the grief-charred
ashes flaked on the fireplace floor after
a night that started with dusk and you

checking your watch, and the dark
that kept deepening after that, or
the uneaten dinner, the knife still

stuck in the uncut loaf of bread
that was bound to go stale, or the burn
of the air as it passed under the door

right before you opened it and started
your own road away from me, from us.
And no, not because of that.

And yes, because of that.

What Started as Fun

something to get you out of the house,
now turns you upside down, hangs
you like a bat who can only
radar himself through life.

It was going to be a fling. Some
handsome stranger who looked good
in his profile pic. Brown eyes, warm
as the coffee you sipped at your first

meeting, when he told you up front
he was looking for something casual.
His fingers curved around a Styrofoam cup,
and you wondered what that hand

would look like on your breast. Now
three months in, and he calls less often,
says things like "busy "or "too
attached." And right there in your kitchen,

as you stand at the sink and wait
for him to text you back, you touch
your own breast, remember how
he loved its warmth. You hear

the word "casual" ringing like
a bell in a distant churchyard.

Bleed

She walks on the sand,
jagged shell pieces cut her,
making her bleed like her last
gone lover, who had held her heart
to his ear to see if he could hear
the ocean. What he heard
was plenty—eel scream,
shark grunt, and everything
she was trying to keep silent.
He liked to see her on Thursdays.
He liked the wild sounds of her secret
shell heart. Liked it and liked it,
and one day got bored. Told himself
these sounds were like the click
of handcuffs, the slam of a prison door.
There were kinder ways to cut himself free,
but what did it matter? What's a little blood
when there's a whole world out there
waiting, and anyway, isn't it
her job to watch where she steps?

When Charley Goes James Dean on Me

He tries, he really does,
and in the summer twilight,
he leans on a stranger's car,
near perfect angle, smoke angels
rising above his head.

You don't smoke, Charley,
I tell him, but he's too deep
in character now. He simply sneers
and flicks the lighted butt into
the street. I want to leave,

but the smell of his leather jacket,
the warm crunch of it, pulls me in.
Charley is holding me now, I can feel
him face up to the moonless sky,
and I start to wonder what I am

supposed to do? Turn him into
my lap, stroke his hair, like I'm Natalie Wood?
And before I can answer, the car owner
shows up. Stares Charley dead in the eyes.
Charley stares back. Chicken run. I hold
what's left of my breath, and just like that,
Charley lights up another smoke.

Wife

Another day of staring out
the window. Maybe she's thinking
what to make for dinner or what
to do with her life. It was different
on the way here. The pre-engagement
flutters, the waiting for the ring.
Life was one big carnival then,
Ferris wheel climbing her up to
the sky, tickle of birdfeather
rushing past her ear. List
of important things: what to wear
to look sexy, ten ways to turn on
a man. Sex, too, was magical,
the moves they discovered together,
replaying them after he left. But
love, like any bird, gets tired of
flying and looks for a place to nest.
So one day, he pulls out a ring and
they soar for a while with wedding plans
and guest lists, maybe even talk of a child.
It's all enough until one day, she starts
replaying it after he leaves for work.
List of important things: shopping, laundry,
letting someone know you're alive. Her
life itself, small as the space inside a wedding
ring, or the width of a tired eye looking
out the window and up at the sky.

That was the Summer

I pretended to be a mermaid, sexless
siren at seven years old. I imagined
I had streaming, black hair, and my legs
flipped together as one. You were
also a mermaid, dark enchantress
of the deeper waters. You led an army
of angry seahorses that were always
ready to pounce. I remind my mother
about that now, though she doesn't
know me anymore. I tell her how you
called last week out of nowhere, and
how this is the summer I will become
some ancient memory you are hoping
to revive. Back in town with your third
husband, showing him what you escaped.
When you called, you asked how everything
was, and how the second grade turned
out. You wanted to know why I never left,
and wasn't I curious about the world. By
world, I assumed you meant your three
husbands and the fourth you will, most
likely, have.

When you left as a kid, it was sudden,
and I kept on waiting for you to call.
I cried to my mother for weeks, a month,
a year. Now, I watch my mother, sitting
helpless in her wheelchair, leaving me
just the same. I spoon tapioca into
her little girl mouth. I tell her you're
back, and I ask if she remembers you
at all. When I say your name, she
just lights up, *evil mermaid,* she
says with perfect recall.

Give Me Back

my childhood. I'd know how to use
it now. This time, I'd savor the sun
thumping down each night like a pink
Spauldeen. And give me back seventh
grade, Mitchell Gorstein, all those silly
minutes I wasted, waiting for him to
notice me. Turns out, he was thinking
of Judy in the third row. Give me back
those achy nights in high school when
I cried for hours over Bobby Traub. How
he dumped me because I wouldn't sneak
out. Give me back how I screamed it
all on my mother. Better yet, give
me back my mother. And give me back
the night I told my husband, the one
man who finally loved me, that he
wasn't enough, and that I found
someone who was. Give me back
his broken face, his broken heart.
No better yet, don't. But most of all,
give me back one morning, any morning,
glittering like Christmas, my future
wrapped in boxes waiting to be opened,
tissue paper and possibility waiting
to rise up like the just-woken sun.

Other Charlies

I come from a long line of Charlies, Charley says. *Like Chaplin and Parker,* he winks. He is all puffed up

with lineage. I half expect him to break into bebop or canewaddle across the floor. *There are other Charlies,*

I remind him. *Like Manson and Sheen. Anyhow, you don't even spell it the same.*

Are you like them?

I could answer that myself—the crazy-eye nights, other nights gauzy with booze. I think of my own

other Charlies, who also spelled their names different— Martin. And David. And Steve.

There's a DNA that passes down from love to love, it shows up in the pulling apart of my heart.

So yeah, Charley, you come from a long line. But not a line that went straight. Just spun around

like an old LP, vinyl and ancient. Like a silent movie reel, twirling around in the flickering dark.

Then

is a memory of sweet canned peas, meatloaf
and the storms that were swirling in my father,
the men pretending to be gentlemen and slicing
my father's sad throat, taking his house, his
manhood and leaving my mother to wrap
cups and saucers in old newspaper, placing
each one gently into the movers' barrels.
She was a soldier, head of her own brigade.
Marching us into the years that followed,
tiny cheap apartment and asking us to dream
smaller. Be patient, she would say, your
father is a good man, and one day the sun
will shine in him. It was hard for me, young
girl, to believe it. I would look at the other fathers,
their golf cart smoothness, their Saturday morning
smiles. They most likely went off to work each
Monday, maybe even taking away houses with
their soft voices, their shoes leaving footprints
like the ones that stayed on my father's back.

Mother-in-Law

We never met. I knew you only
from his voice hunching up
with your name. His first loss.
Each autumn, on the anniversary,
he'd light a thick candle, let it burn
into another year you wouldn't have.
I once saw him sob for a woman
on TV whose cancer, like yours, wouldn't heal.
When we visited the school where you taught,
I watched as he stood and stood by a tree
with your name. By now, you know

he's remarried. Children and all.
On nights like this, just past summer,
air crisp as apple-skin, you and I
almost meet. There we are, in a swirl
of thought just above his head.
You, with your dress the color of wrong
sunlight that funerals sometimes have, and me
tinged with the shade of faint regret
that the once-loved always wear.
The two of us transparent, real
as breath, our hands about to touch.

Flight

It was the trees he noticed
way up high, how different

they looked from this angle. First time
flying? I asked, though I knew him

for a newbie right off. And then,
of course, the mountains, topped off

with snow, and could he just grab
a handful? I told him no, we're on a schedule,

and besides, the birds don't do that.
Amateur stuff. Agreed, he said,

then lit up at the sight of the ocean below,
and did we have time to dive in? Here's

where I mention he's been looking down
the entire time, and is this what I can expect?

Here's where I also ask him
if he even gets the point of flight.

Pumpkin School

Man stands in a pumpkin patch,
how he got there, no idea. But
his mind last night was a strangle
of thoughts—the firing, the kitchen
knife his wife came *this* close
to using. And later, the whiskey
at *Lenny's Dip and Dive* and good
old Ray who was able to drive
because the booze was killin'
his ticker, y'know?

                       But now, Man
stands alone in a pumpkin patch,
highest thing there, and by all
accounts, the smartest. Figures
he'll tell these bobble heads a thing
or two about life. But first, he needs
to take a piss. *This is the real lesson,*
he reckons. One day, you're fine,
and the next, life is aiming its dick
at your head.

            Now, old Ray
pulls up to the patch, honkin'
and hollerin' how Man's old lady
has been calling and also his boss.
But Man waves Ray off, takes
another look at the pumpkins.
Poor bastards, he thinks, up
to their necks in earthdirt, unlike
him, the one with the legs that he
can aim in any direction he wants.

Probably

That summer was knobby
and loose-skinned like the knuckles
of a tired old man. My father
had up and left us. Walked out
after dinner and became part
of the dark. My mother bent
into herself, baby-like, never
quite straightening up. The sky
unloaded the same rain each day
at 3 o'clock. Up went the silly
umbrellas that didn't keep anything
dry. The lines on my mother's face
grew deeper, and pain glowed through
her like radium.

                And probably,
my father was holed up in a cheap motel,
flickering vacancy sign. He might have been
reading the newspaper, circling the want
ads or ads for a whole new family.
Later he might have looked out
the window, bloodshot sunset
across the motel court and later
still, most likely, sitting alone, he was
probably drinking a toast to himself.

Dusk

and the sun becomes nothing.
Air hissing out like a beach ball,
collapsing at the horizon. I remember
my mother telling me it was illusion,

that the sun stayed still, and it was
the earth turning away. I didn't
believe her. If the earth were spinning,

I said, I would have been knocked down
flat. She didn't answer, but disappeared
into the next room. Now, it is years later,
afternoon nursing home, and I still don't

trust my mother. I don't believe her empty
eyes, her flaccid mouth that can't even say
my name. I am watching her sink into
the horizon, her life flattened, her death
waiting to blow up like a beach ball
and send her hissing out of my sight

while I remain left behind, unmothered
now, and spinning in place.

Charley Gives Me an Either/Or

as in, I either buy him a horse
or he's outta here. I'm so used

to this love salad. Dice up some
heartbreak, toss in a threat, and voila!

Dinner is served. Only me? I'm more
of an *a la mode*. Love so sweet, it's topped

with sweeter. Not some crazy goop where
he orders a horse he won't even ride. I think

he likes the sound of it—hoof clop and stall muck.
Much the way he liked the sound of love, until

he realized he would have to start paying attention.
So yeah, I'm not gonna buy him a horse. Unless,

of course, I do. Till then, I'll watch the days
sand dribble away, until I see him pouring oats

in a bucket and waiting for me to snuffle and neigh
my own self, if that's what it comes down to.

When We Meet Up at the Parker Avenue Grill

The two of us sit there, waiting to unpeel
the night. Giant awkward orange.
You are loaded with a story; it
is a fish thrashing around in your
pelican beak. I am thinking you should
swallow it like any real pelican would
do. It is the story, I know, of your other
woman, the one whose scarf I found
when I was cleaning your car. When
I was doing something nice for you,
hoping it might fix us.

I like to think I am safe,
but the truth is I dive
in the deep parts. I like to stare
into the ocean's blue face and rip
apart its skin. That's how I found
you, remember? The footprints
of your last woman still fresh
on the ground around you. And now,
I am that woman, about to have
my heart wrapped up and handed back.

We order light—BLT's and coffee—
and before I can stop it, the story
has wriggled its fishtail out
of your opening mouth. A thumbnail
has broken the night's orange skin,
the sudden sting of citrus filling up the air.

I Think of My Mother

when youth was her best
accessory, when she's standing

on the dance floor, beautiful and alone.
She is waiting there

in black and white, the way
I have seen her in photographs.

Right about now, my father
comes in, nervous

and white-faced as the moon.
Of course, he, too, is posed,

his better side
pushed forward in my mind.

Only this time, there is something
I haven't seen before;

maybe it's the August heat
that is making him sweat,

or the curve
of my mother's right hip

as she stands there, swaying
in place. He is wearing

the look of a man
who's convinced

he may never think straight again.
Dumbstruck, until

the music thuds him on the back
like an older brother,

when he takes that first
step towards her

and I am about to begin.

Daughter in the Kitchen

is watching her mother whose eyes
are windowed with tears. *Damn onions*,
the mother says, but the daughter knows
better. She knows that the tears are for
the husband/father who left last week,
who took his cufflinks, his clothing,
but mostly his scent. The daughter doesn't
know yet how she will be sniffing the necks
of men her entire life for her father's cologne,
the starch of a crisp white shirt. The mother,
on the other hand, is very aware and has taken
to cooking to clog up the air. Her hand doming
an onion now, the knife moving swiftly. The
mother sniffing back tears. The daughter
standing by and watching the onion give way
like the soft skin of a heart.

Roses

Charley buys me three and even
names them—Agnes, Brunhilde, and Pearl.

I tell him flowers don't live long enough
for names, and he just winks and says,

like love. Maybe he's thinking our love
went nameless long ago, and these flowers
are marking its grave. No matter.
I like the aroma, the red, red fullness.

I put them in a vase, and they spread
apart. They look like the top of the asterisk

I might someday put next to Charley's
name. *Yeah*, it would say, *he was
technically my lover, but really that
was me being broken.* Later that week,

when the roses droop into the asterisk's
bottom half, Charley says I depressed

them, especially Agnes, and couldn't I
please be happy for once? I promise
to try harder, and when the girls finally die,
turn into rosecrumble scattered on the floor.

I sweep it up quick so no one has to see
the mess. Like love, I want to tell Charley,
almost exactly like love.

In My Poems, Sometimes I Have Children

Daughters mostly, because I know
their routines. Flatirons and tampons.
To invent boys, I would need to ask
questions, learn to talk sports.
In my poems, sometimes,
my children appreciate
me. Pretend daughter Fiona,
says things like *Mom, if it weren't*
for you, I'd be living in an essay
for crying out loud. She's right.
If I were a made-up child, I
would prefer the crinoline
swish of a simile, so much kinder
than the hard angles of non-fiction.
A pretend son wouldn't be so generous.
He would say he's a lie I tell
myself to feel better about what
I haven't done. I would laugh at him.
Pretend mothers can do that.
Then I would sit him down
and tell him my poems aren't lies at all.
They're just the truths that didn't happen.

My Sister is Dying

and not because she wants to,
and not because we didn't know
about death, but we always thought
it was for other people, like our crazy
drunk neighbor who smashed his car
and was talked about in whispers after that.
But now, my sister lives alone in a house
that holds her like it's a giant mouth,
and she is just a word it wants to say.
She's widowed, and her children are grown
and gone. She's too young to be this old,
and so she flirts with sickness the way
she used to flirt with boys. Pills and
joint aches fight off the loneliness that
stares at her like she's a giant television.
She keeps telling me that death is near.
Syrupy slow but coming. I want to say she's
wrong, that things are not always as they
seem, that it turns out our neighbor wasn't
drunk, but rather had a heart attack, and that
the stink was lifted off his death. I want to say
it's okay to be cool, to treat death like it's a boy
we know will call, but it might be good

to play a little hard to get.

Love was Okay

until one day, it wasn't. Charley started
to fidget with words like boring and change.

Even kissing me became too much like work,
and he stopped showing up. So me, I quit

lipstick and high heels because why waste
the pretty, as teen-aged me would say.

That took some explaining to little-girl
me who loves a misty perfume, the flower

of a twirly skirt. I told her shh, this isn't
forever. Count to a hundred, find a safe

spot on the wall. Pretend the night isn't
a long black carpet unspooling as Charley

snores up most of the air, his chest like
a mountain, then a valley, then a mountain.

Fish Story

Pretend you don't see the photo
hung up in the hallway, the one of you
and your father fishing where he dangles
his catch from his scratchy hands. Later,
he would tell the neighbors how the fish
was so much bigger than it looked. The same
way he would tell you the moon is hanging
in the sky just for you, and when you grow
up you can choose the nights it will shine.
Pretend you weren't angry
when you did grow up and wished
the moon away those final hospital nights
where your father gasped like
a dying fish, and the moon prying in
the window which was framing the night
like an unpeopled photograph where
you could shout and shout about
that time you stood knee deep in that
long-ago lake, and your father
promised you he would live forever.

Even in the Shark World

there are rules, laws about
sleepswimming and razorteeth
and what the sharkbelly wants.
Like my father and his own rules,
laws for his kingdom, our tiny
apartment with the neighbors' footsteps
pattering above, a layer of interruption
between my father and God.
I remember my father shaking
his fist at the ceiling. *Aren't you
listening*? he would say, his fish mouth
opening and closing with tired, unheard
words. *You just gotta stop.*
I was never sure who he was yelling at,
the neighbors with their muffled shuffling,
or the God who my father swore was always
testing him. Either way, I wanted him to let go,
let the ocean glide him forward, be like
those sharks who keep moving
even with speargashes in their skin.
Forget about the neighbors, forget
about God. Remember only survival
and keeping your eyes fixed on the food fish
up ahead of you, rather than the harpoon
boats hovering above that are more likely
to get you once you are standing still.

Shark Week!

Oh yes! Shark TV!
    Gorgeous fishmachines,
teeth big as a man's thumb.

They glide without apology,
    while you, poor soul, fight
your wife for the remote.

You really *mean* to live your life,
    get off the couch
and release your heartswallows,

let them whir their wings
    and beat you senseless
with everything you want to do.

You would grab your wife, who is sitting
    tea-cozy still, but right now
there's a Great White on the tube.

Torpedo-sure, he moves
    towards food, which could be anything—
a boot, a fish, a man.

And look! Some crazy bastard
    has mounted a whale carcass
while frenzied sharks try to shake

him loose. *Anything for a photo*,
    he says. He's a thousand times
alive, and you can't help but hope

he falls, that the sharks take him
    in one delicious gulp.
Aren't you glad that isn't me?

you ask your wife, who looks back
    dead-stare, asking if sharkgobble
is worse than other way to die?

Worse than, let's say,
    watching your life disappear
one unremarkable night at a time.

When Charley Starts to Look Like the Weather

it is winter. Trees, bare down to
branchfingers. Halo of almost snow

in the sky. Charley has gone tundra.
Air around him, a frosty cloud.

When he opens his mouth, it's the gargle
of spinning tires. *Try to dig yourself*

out, I want to say. *Tell me this isn't
working.* If only I could read his paper

heart, I wouldn't need to hear him say
the words. His face tells me nothing. I've

learned to not even look. I settle in
to wait for spring. Slow, steady thaw,

but by then he might have slipped
away, leaving only his body behind,

melting like a snowman sinking slowing into itself.

Years Later

I think of my mother, gone now, how
we'd shop and then stop at *Adrian's Bakery*
because rye bread was special. We would
walk into that hum, that click of tickets,
and take a number for our turn. My mother

would order, *just half a loaf*, she would say,
sliced. The clerk didn't like it—*who's
gonna buy the other half?*

I would watch the knife cut into that pregnant
bread belly, aroma filling the air like a baby.
This was my mother in the real world, not like
at home, where she napped when she could,
waiting all night for my father.

And then the clerk, handing her the crumpled
white bag. My mother taking her small victory.
I would take one more breath of that breadsexy
air, follow my mother out the door, and watch
her already starting to shrink.

Question for Jessica

Why wait, when the December moon
comes only once a year? Instead, you bundle
closer to the man you are trying

to quit. You trace the fist-print
with your finger, the finger
you dialed the cops with, then changed

your moon-fickle mind. Tomorrow,
your man will want breakfast,
having slept all night, while you stared

at the door. Maybe you can kill
the anger. Sigh enough
times and it starts to feel

like breath. You'll call me for comfort.
I'll say, come over, you can stay here.
I got all the room in the world

since my own man left. But you,
you have a different plan. You hit
the street, sun over easy in the sky.

You got it figured out, and leaving him
is too easy. This is what you'll tell me,
coffee scalding your tongue.

On your way home, you'll see a homeless girl,
curled like a question. Quarter? She'll ask
and you give it to her if she swears

to no booze. *And no men*, you think.
You will turn to leave, but your eye will stop
on her bruiseless skin.

And just for the splittest
of seconds, you'll wish
you were that girl.

Poem Where Charley Gets It in the Gut

Not even time is on his side. In fact,
it's what ultimately gets him, slackens

that perfect jaw, pouches those blue, blue eyes.
Yes, Charley, it hurts, this admitting you're no

longer young, but let's face it, now, you are
even with the rest of us. Yeah, your boybrain

still tricks you into thinking you could fuck
the waitress if it weren't for me. You do

the lustmath in your head—you, minus me,
equals the life you *really* want—

madcap and motorcycle dangerous all at
the same time. I can almost hear you

thinking of the ways you could exit our table,
how you'd wink the waitress to meet you

out back. But really, Charley, I am
sitting here, watching your fingers,

puffy and pink, curled a bit too hard
around your coffee cup. Me, weighted

with patience, and you trying to grab
this young woman's attention for a second,

if only to ask for the check.

For Barbara

Just when it looks like the sun
will always roll out like a long
yellow carpet, the wind shifts,
rubs clouds against the sky
till they shred and break

with news from a friend down South.
She writes of her strip of Carolina
beach, a margin between her and the sea,

where she can be found most mornings walking
off her mother's recent death. It still makes
no sense, the ships falling off the horizon,
the swimmer, one mile out, taking breath

for granted. But it's sand that puzzles her
most, particles so small, she wouldn't miss
a single one, yet now it's all she's got to stand on.

So, I have to wonder, she closes, how solid anything is
when the wind can pick it up at whim, the waves repeating
the story that sounds different every time, and the swimmer
pulled further, not feeling the water's slow advance,
how he doesn't suspect a thing.

Status

Another day since Charley left.
Status: *Still feeling out of water.*
No one comments. No one likes.
I know Charley would get it.
He may be gone, but we're still friends.
When I check his page, his profile picture smiles
at me, like that day we went to the lake.
That's when love was easy as swimming fish,
natural and oozy-smooth.
Charley said that fish have their own network.
Invisible. Watersong. Just like me and him.
Later that night, we gutted and fried up
the trout that Charley caught. It snapped
and bucked in the buttersizzle.
Charley said he liked that not even death
could hold it down. Next morning,
Charley left. Something about *where is he?*
Where is he going?
Status, he said, unsure, but looking,
and I needed to swim out of his way.
Which I did, but sometimes now
I still hear him.
Some leftover fish language
that only I could hear.
Maybe a "sorry" or "there was
no other way." That's okay, I joke
to myself. "There's plenty
like him out there in the sea."
A joke is what I want to believe
that I know isn't true.

Status: You are going on without me.
Status: I am singing your name into the air.

On My Way Away

from you, an Iowa cornfield
and I passed each other. Me,
in my beat-up Chevy, heading
for the coast, and the cornfield
stuck on its earthplate. I watched
the cornstalks nodding in the just-dusk
breeze. You really *were* an asshole,
they were saying, or maybe that's
what I wanted to hear. It was late
June, and elsewhere, the bees
were sticky with flowersex, working
the pistils of hopeful roses that
might have been wishing the bees
would stay the night. I kept moving,
and by the time I made it to Cali,
I had eaten an entire country.
I thought of you way back east,
staring at the ghost-me I left
behind, the only picture of you
I would keep from now on, the
one where finally you
are the thing standing still.

Charley Leaves Me in a Swamp

not a real swamp, a love swamp,
full of alligator syrup and tropical

glop. I am halfway between ooze
and goo. But Charley doesn't care.

He's always known he could break me
down to parts, pull off my hands,

which are now on the floor, fingerpuddles
on the woodstain. My feet have snapped

off and walked themselves over
to the trash. The rest of me is leftover

mess, arms and legs and torso splayed
out on the bed, and yet, my head

is screaming, think positive. This could
get better. Charley could return, love

me back to solid ground. But meantime,
I just have to be patient, maybe look

up at the ceiling, at the light bulb
shining like a hazy sunbubble

which perhaps if I wait long enough
might even give me a tan.

Café *Crazy*

Where the stink of old perfume drowns out
the coffee aroma. Where the hurt girls go
to watch their loves die. It's a slow death,
Ruby will tell you. She's the day waitress,
and man, she's seen it all. Old women with
their walnut bodies who gave their lusty husbands
one more chance, and others with a crush of dried
petals that they just kept holding onto. Ruby wipes
down the counter, lets the women rant and choke
love by its scrawny little neck.

                        It's Friday afternoon,
prime time for heartache. All the men who said
they'd call, and Saturday's looking to be one long
and lonely bitch. The door swings open, and three
girls sulk in, swollen eyes and new to these parts.
Ruby simply flicks them the onceover. And when
they sit down at the counter, she doesn't bother
with a menu. She knows exactly what they'll have.

About the Author

Francine Witte is the author of the poetry chapbooks *Only, Not Only* (Finishing Line Press, 2012) and *First Rain* (Pecan Grove Press, 2009), winner of the Pecan Grove Press competition, and the flash fiction chapbooks *Cold June* (Ropewalk Press*)*, selected by Robert Olen Butler as the winner of the 2010 Thomas A. Wilhelmus Award, and *The Wind Twirls Everything* (MuscleHead Press). Her poetry chapbook, *Not All Fires Burn the Same* won the 2016 Slipstream chapbook contest. She lives in New York City.

www.ingramcontent.com/pod-product-compliance
Lightning Source LLC
LaVergne TN
LVHW021619080426
835510LV00019B/2661